P9-EAX-366

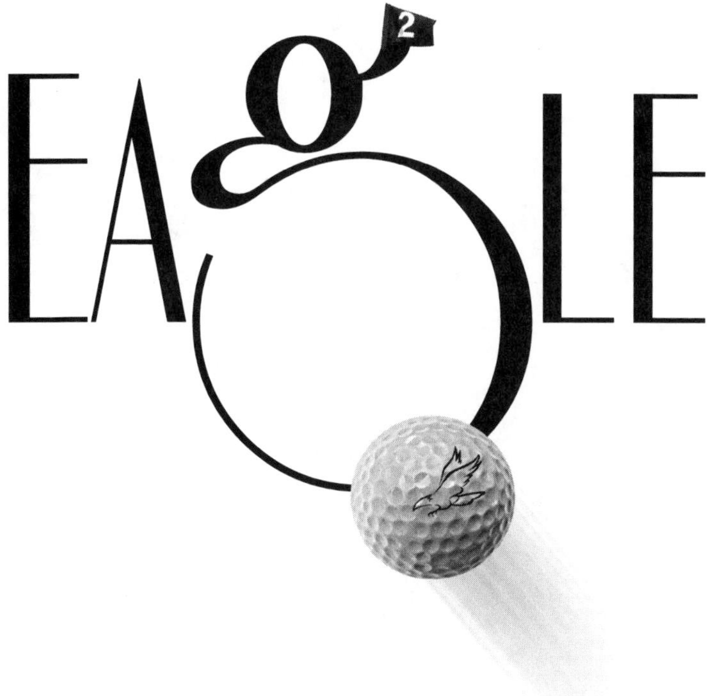
EAGLE
2

CAROLYN SNELLING

CREATION
HOUSE
A STRANG COMPANY

EAGLE by Carolyn Snelling
Published by Creation House
A Strang Company
600 Rinehart Road
Lake Mary, Florida 32746
www.strangbookgroup.com

Unless otherwise noted, all Scripture quotations
are from the Holy Bible, New International
Version of the Bible. Copyright © 1973, 1978, 1984,
International Bible Society. Used by permission.

Design Director: Bill Johnson
Cover design by Justin Evans

Library of Congress Control Number: 2009927900
International Standard Book Number:
978-1-59979-851-6

First Edition

10 11 12 13 14 — 987654321
Printed in the United States of America

DEDICATION

*Praise the Lord, O my soul, and
forget not all his benefits—who
forgives all your sins and heals all
your diseases, who redeems your
life from the pit and crowns you
with love and compassion, who
satisfies your desires with good
things so that your youth is renewed
like the eagle's.*

PSALM 103:2–5

CONTENTS

PREFACE

THE GAME OF golf can completely consume a life. In addition to playing the game, countless hours are spent on the driving range and on the practice putting green. Untold hours are given over to perusing a plethora of golf magazines, and more time still is spent watching infomercials on the latest in golf gadgetry. All these activities are the means to an end, the golfer's ultimate quest— lowering his or her score or being under par.

My husband, Bob, will go to a golf store just so he can hold the latest club, check out the gear, or talk shop with a salesclerk.

Of course, who could overlook watching the golf pros on television, something I affectionately refer to as "golfer altar calls." This endeavor can eat up an entire day if the TiVo or DVR is not set to record.

Let's not forget actual playing time for the casual golfer, which could mean a minimum of four hours, not to mention travel time to and from the golf course.

All this, and I haven't discussed the monetary

investment in the clothing, the equipment, and the cost of playing. It is a hobby run amok.

As I mentioned, the golfer has one goal in mind with this type of emotional, monetary, and personal investment, lowering his or her next golf score or bringing it under par. In golf, the under-par terms are *birdie* and *eagle*.[1]

If an eagle will dramatically change a round of golf, how would living each day under par as Christians change our lives? As a born-again Christian, I can't say that I have always made an under-par investment in living my life for Christ. Have you?

Regrettably and with the most profound shame, I confess that I have at times not allowed Christ to consume my life the way golf can for passionate golfers. Yes, writing about Him consumes my days, but how am I with others when I am away from my keyboard? More often than not, I feel like such a hypocrite. Isn't there an adage about how those who can't do, teach? Well, maybe in my case it should be, those who can't do, write.

> Then he began to call down curses on himself and he swore to them, "I don't

---

1   A birdie is when a golfer takes one less shot than the prescribed number on a particular golf hole. An eagle is two shots less than the prescribed number.

> know the man!" Immediately a rooster
> crowed. Then Peter remembered the word
> Jesus had spoken: "Before the rooster
> crows, you will disown me three times."
> And he went outside and wept bitterly.
> —MATTHEW 26:74–75

While I cannot imagine denying Christ, I
wonder how much of a slippery slope I tread when
I don't make a commitment to live a life in Him.
He has told us what He holds dear, and I seem, at
times, to fail miserably.

> "Teacher, which is the greatest com-
> mandment in the Law?" Jesus replied:
> "'Love the Lord your God with all your
> heart and with all your soul and with all
> your mind.' This is the first and greatest
> commandment. And the second is like
> it: 'Love your neighbor as yourself.'"
> —MATTHEW 22:36–39

While my writing is meant to honor God, it
brings my bogeys[2], or the times I mess up, into

---

2 A bogey occurs when a golfer goes over the number of prescribed shots by one
on any given hole of golf. Bogeys contribute to an over-par score—something all
golfers dread!

plain view. There are days and moments when I think, *Am I the only one who can't seem to get it right for Christ?*

This book is written to highlight attributes of people I have witnessed who are under par for God, and it is my prayer that if you struggle as I do perhaps together we can learn from these "under-par" people and create our own "eagle" flight patterns.

As many times as I fail, I know I want to soar like an eagle for Him. Don't you?

> Even youths grow tired and weary, and young men stumble and fall; but those who hope in the LORD will renew their strength. They will soar on wings like eagles; they will run and not grow weary, they will walk and not be faint.
>
> —ISAIAH 40:30–31

ACKNOWLEDGMENTS

FOR GOD

Praise the LORD, O my soul; all my inmost being, praise his holy name.

—PSALM 103:1

FOR MY HUSBAND, BOB

Strengthen me with raisins, refresh me with apples, for I am faint with love.

—SONG OF SONGS 2:5

FOR NANCY

Pleasant words are a honeycomb, sweet to the soul and healing to the bones.

—PROVERBS 16:24

FOR PASTOR BILL BARLEY AND HIS LIVING STONES STAFF

You also, like living stones, are being built into a spiritual house to be a holy priesthood, offering spiritual sacrifices acceptable to God through Jesus Christ.

—1 PETER 2:5

FOR PASTOR LEE MCFARLAND AND HIS RADIANT CHURCH STAFF

Those who look to him are radiant; their faces are never covered with shame. This poor man called, and the LORD heard him; he saved him out of all his troubles.

—PSALM 34:5–6

FOR THE CHILDREN IN MY LIFE: JENNIFER, STACY, BRIAN, CAMERON, CHELSEA, AUSTIN, MONIQUE, AND KATHRYN

I have no greater joy than to hear that my children are walking in the truth.

—3 JOHN 4

FOR MY STRANG COMMUNICATIONS/ CREATION HOUSE FAMILY

I thank my God every time I remember you. In all my prayers for all of you, I always pray with joy because of your partnership in the gospel from the first day until now, being confident of this, that he who began a good work in you will carry it on to completion until the day of Christ Jesus.

—PHILIPPIANS 1:3–6

FOR MY ANONYMOUS FRIEND IN "THE FINISHING HOLE"

"I have told you these things, so that in me you may have peace. In this world you will have trouble. But take heart! I have overcome the world."

—JOHN 16:33

INTRODUCTION

N*ICHE MARKETING.* T*HIS* is a term the book trade uses when an author writes a series of books based on a particular theme.

Imagine my surprise when the team at Strang Communications agreed I should consider writing follow-up stories to my first book, *Mulligan: A Second Chance at True Love and God's Grace.* Mind you, my new publishing family didn't know if *Mulligan* would be a success with you, the reader, or the trade. But the folks at Strang have a singular purpose in mind when they publish books, and that is to lead people to Christ.

My husband, Bob, and I met the Creation House team, the co-publishing arm of Strang Communications, in August 2008. That's the time of year when we Arizonans try to escape what we lovingly refer to as our dry heat in search of more favorable climates. In our infinite wisdom, Bob and I chose Florida, the antithesis of dry heat. For those of you who may not know, Florida in August is best described as a sticky, "can't wait to take a shower

1

as soon as you walk outside" kind of wet heat. We wanted, however, to meet the team that would bring you *Mulligan*, and this was the best time for all involved.

I found a pretty good rate for airfare, reserved a hotel using our accumulated points, and rented a compact car, the type with the manual door locks and window handles. I prayed it would stay on the road if we encountered any gusty weather. We decided to splurge using our AAA discount and buy a two-day park hopper pass to Walt Disney World, one of our most favorite places on Earth!

Now, being a white-knuckle flyer, I was amazed I made it across the country without having thoughts of our plane crashing. Did you ever see the movie *French Kiss* with Meg Ryan? Do you recall her character and how terrified she was to fly? Well, that depicts me to a "tee."

Regrettably, I have allowed satan and his minions to bring about the worst in my thoughts when I fly. I always carry my Student Bible and iPod loaded with Christian music on board, and you would think those items would be all the spiritual armor I would need to fight any battles. Thankfully, on the flight to Orlando I allowed them to work for me. I also believe my thoughts were powered by the idea that if I were on my way to sign a contract to write a book about God, surely He wouldn't allow anything bad to happen to us.

When we landed safely at the Orlando International Airport, I said my thanks to Him and our adventure began. The Orlando airport is very user-friendly and well marked, making it easy for a visitor to get around. The airport shopping and food court include a wide array of choices for every budget and taste. The rental car representative at the airport was especially pleasant, told some jokes, gave us a map, and drove us safely to the rental agency. After we signed our life away for our rental car—gee whiz, the contracts are like giving up your firstborn—we hit the road. The only visitor drawbacks while traveling in Florida are the road signs and tolls. I am certain Bob and I overlooked a tollbooth on one of the highways, as we didn't realize until it was too late that we were in something called a Sun Pass lane. To the transportation division of the City of Orlando: please send us a bill for the fifty-cent toll!

We arrived at our hotel pleasantly surprised by our ability to find it without too many in-car rerouting suggestions from the navigator, a.k.a., me. We inquired at the front desk as to a recommendation of a nearby restaurant where we could eat dinner. Our desk clerk was extremely helpful, making several very agreeable suggestions. We finally settled on a fresh fish establishment. Remember, we are from land-locked Arizona, and our "fresh fish" is always frozen!

We had an incredible meal, a great night's sleep, and we awoke early the next morning ready to successfully locate Lake Mary, home to Strang Communications.

Lake Mary, Florida, was recently voted in a CNN poll among the top five best places to live. It boasts a population of 13,200 and is but half an hour's drive from Orlando and about forty-five minutes from Daytona Beach. Believe it or not, we got pretty good directions from MapQuest, and I am happy to report we were early for our one o'clock appointment. Once again, we went in search of food. I don't know what it is when Bob and I travel domestically; we must think we are going to a third-world country instead of the United States, as we are always in search of and seemingly worried about getting our next meal.

After our fast-food delight, we arrived at the three-story-high Strang building. Upon entering the finely appointed yet in no way ostentatious lobby, we felt as if the message being relayed to visitors was, "We are doing God's business, and we will be respectful."

We were greeted by a bright-faced, bespectacled, well-dressed man with a happy cadence. He introduced himself as Allen Quain. He led us through the Strang corridors and to the elevator that would lift us to his office. On the way to the elevators, we passed the bookstore that houses all the Strang family books. I allowed my thoughts to wander. Would God allow *Mulligan* to join such a prestigious library?

As we rode in the elevator, I was intrigued by Allen's Southern drawl and asked its origin. He emigrated from North Carolina to Florida and shared with us that he was an ordained minister. I asked if he wanted us to call him Pastor Allen, and he said, "No, I am just Allen." He introduced us to his awesome staff. I had spoken with some of them already via e-mail and felt as if I were reuniting with old friends. Allen took us into his humble office, surrounded by all the Strang family books. He gave us a couple of those books so we could see the quality of the production. Of course, we were totally impressed.

Suddenly I felt embarrassed for my clothes,

wrinkled from the humidity and looking as if I had slept in them. If my mother were still alive, she would have cringed seeing me in such an unkempt state. I found myself trying to use my cotton shawl to cover my pants. I was hoping, too, that Allen wouldn't notice my upper lip sweating profusely. I know my nerves were a result of the circumstances, the humidity, and of course the by then common hot flash!

I wanted to cry at God's generosity toward me but knew I needed to keep it together. I had just met Allen, for heaven's sake, and I didn't want him to think I was unprofessional.

I joked with him if *Mulligan*, my story about God giving me a second chance at true love in the form of my second husband, Bob, made it to the big screen, I wanted Angelina Jolie to play my role. Talk about getting ahead of myself! Obviously, I was nervous and didn't know what to say. I expected Bob to back me up, as he always does in stressful moments, and offer up Anthony Hopkins or Richard Gere or some other debonair and mature Hollywood hottie to play his role. Instead, he said, "If Angelina plays you, I get to play me, right?" We laughed. It was all very surreal that we would even be laughing about such a possibility.

Allen and his team were incredibly gracious, professional, and nothing short of fantastic. We told them we were going to go to Disney World, and they gave us some great tips as to the parades we needed to see and restaurants we needed to visit. They must have known about our secret quest for our next meal. I felt so blessed in that moment that God brought these amazing people into my life. I, once again, wanted to cry, but thought better of it.

After our meeting, as Bob and I were walking toward our econo-car, I said to him, "I have an idea for a second book." At the time I had no idea about niche marketing. "Let's get *Mulligan* situated first, shall we?" Bob suggested. Of course, he was right, although I thought I had a great idea. The book would be titled *Fifty Before Fifty*, referencing fifty things we all should do before we turn fifty. There would be Scripture references and some questions I thought would be important for you, the reader, to answer.

"Don't tell Allen," Bob joked, "or you might scare him off." Looking back now, I realize those were probably fifty things I wanted to hear as I created a wish list of places to see or things to do.

I was totally barking up the wrong tree. Like many things in my life, I was trying to create something that was all about me.

When we left the Strang team, we went back to the hotel to mull over the contract and to spend a couple of days at Disney. We covered every inch of Epcot, Magic Kingdom, and Disney's Hollywood Studios. We got caught in a major downpour while we were at one of the parks and bought a couple of those great ponchos Disney sells to keep off the rain. We had a great adventure, but by the end of a few days we were longing for our Arizona monsoons—go figure. Anyway, in the meantime I put the idea of a second book to rest.

A couple of weeks after we returned home, I received a book in the mail from Allen's team called *Guerrilla Marketing for Writers: 100 Weapons for Selling Your Work*.[3] This book gives new authors a lot of marketing ideas and suggestions to help their books succeed. Let's face it, though, if God wants certain people to benefit from reading something, they will, regardless of what we authors hope will happen or try to make happen. But, since Allen and his team thought the book had merit, I felt at

---

3 Jay Levinson, Rick Frishman, and Michael Larsen, *Guerrilla Marketing for Writers* (Cincinnati, OH: Writer's Digest Books, 2001).

the very least I should give it a read. I was well into it when the concept of niche marketing crossed my view.

I sent Allen my idea for this book on September 8, 2008. My mood was somber that day for two reasons. My mom passed away on September 3, 2006, so I am especially sad around early September. Although she accepted Christ in her last days, I still mourn.

About that time of year, I also get a pit in my stomach remembering, as if it were yesterday, the horrific images from September 11. I pray that our country never forgets that fateful day for the sake of those brave souls whose lives were lost and the families and friends left behind. I also pray for the men and women who fight to keep our country free. My thanks to the men and women in uniform. They are true eagles for our country! Let us never forget.

Here is what I sent Allen:

> Although I wrote *Mulligan* to honor God and marriage, it also revealed my unenviable status as a golfing hack. I don't really care about the game, although I will watch a portion of a major tournament on television, but only to spend

time with my wonderful hubby. Thank God for TiVo and DVRs. Stick me with a needle, poke a stick in my eye, but please, please don't ask me to spend four hours playing the game.

So, if indeed the game is so unimportant to me, why on Earth am I so bothered by the expression "not feeling up to par"? I can't get my brain around how it wants to draw a correlation to the term *par* in golf. Yes, I understand the adage refers to *par* as something normal. But what the underlying meaning misses badly is that serious golfers always hope their score will be well under par. After fifteen years of marriage to such a golfer, I have come to understand that par is not all that great. Golfers strive for under-par status, achieved in the form of an eagle or perhaps a birdie, an ace, or even a double-eagle.[4]

As a Christian, does it intrigue you as it does me to pursue this idea that

---

4 An ace is a score of one on any hole but most often usually scored on a par three. A double-eagle is a score of three under par on any hole but most usually scored on a par five.

maybe we should live our lives under par for God? Following in all His ways shouldn't mean treating life as normal or business as usual. The choice we make to freely accept Him in our hearts, our minds, and our souls should give us pause each day to rethink how we embrace our lives. Shouldn't it?

I get impatient with the clerk at the grocery store for not checking me out of line fast enough. Yet do I stop to think how she may not be going home to a husband as loving as mine?

I get angry when a boss gives me grief over a report that missed the mark. Yet do I stop to realize that he may have done me a favor for improving my future reports?

I am fearful of flying in airplanes. Yet do I stop to realize that I am a child of God? Whom shall I fear?

No, too often I do not live my life under par. I do not always soar like an eagle, either. Eagles are creatures that exude a sense of grace. As a Christian, I should recognize that my walk is, indeed, something to be handled in a precious manner. I should take on a flight pattern that exudes grace and a recognition that my God thinks of me as His rare and precious child. He cares for me like no other. He cares for you in that way also. I should treat you that way, too.

This book will reveal eagles I have personally witnessed, how they soar for God, and more importantly, what we can learn from them. We can and should stretch our reach on His behalf in every interaction. I want to be an eagle. I want to be under par for God. Join me as we go for the green in two and take flight for God!

Since I wrote this excerpt, unbelievably and amazingly I have been bitten by the golf bug. Given my previous disdain for the game, how is this possible? Hopefully, the story you are about to read will shed some light on this new development.

God remarkably showed me over and over again within just a two-week timeframe how He wanted this story told. I am amazed at His reminders, and you will be too!

There are three fundamentals associated with golf—balance, focus, and correct alignment with the target. I will use these fundamentals throughout this book as metaphors to show the way toward achieving Christ-consuming, under-par status.

As I give golf and my commitment to Christ a mulligan,[5] let's turn now to the stories of the incredible eagles I have witnessed. I would be willing to guess you will recognize these people as you hear my interaction with them, for everyone knows at least one eagle in their life, or at least I pray you do. They are the unsung heroes that would never expect a word to be written about them.

> Do nothing out of selfish ambition or vain conceit, but in humility consider others better than yourselves. Each of you should look not only to your own interests, but also to the interests of others. Your attitude should be the same as that of Christ Jesus.
>
> —Philippians 2:3–5

---

5 In golf there's a term for a second chance, a mulligan, in which a golfer has the opportunity to retake an errant shot.

chapter 1

BALANCE IS EVERYTHING
A Firm Footing in Christ

I T WAS LATE September 2008, and I was headed
back to school.

Hey, that reminds me of a 1970s song with
similar lyrics sung by rock-and-roll icon Rod
Stewart. Remember his spiky blonde hair and raspy
voice? Maybe you recall the song too, "Maggie
May"? Anyway, I digress.

Before going back to school, however, my
husband, Bob, and I were taking his daughter, our
son-in-law, and our three grandchildren on vacation. It was during this two-week span of time that
God revealed to me His eagles and some pretty
amazing, in-your-face lessons.

I had just finished a seven-month volunteer stint
as the director of operations for Radiant Church.
Although I was thrilled to help until a permanent

replacement was identified, I wanted to finish my doctoral studies; promote my first God-inspired book, *Mulligan: A Second Chance at True Love and God's Grace;* work on the book you are now reading; and spend overdue and much-needed quality time with my husband and our family.

It's funny, as a kid growing up in the 1960s and 1970s, I didn't worry about balance in life. Maybe it was because there weren't as many extracurricular activities then as there are for kids today. If there were, I didn't know about them. It is true, however, that every Saturday—yes, every Saturday—from the time I was twelve until I was eighteen, my mother and I attended meetings of a particular religious social order. My only other balancing act during my teen years was between boys and school. You can probably guess where the majority of my time was spent.

I honestly don't know how my grandsons balance their busy lives, what with playing baseball, high school golf, and basketball, taking guitar lessons, social agendas, playing *Rock Band* or other games with their Wii, oh, and of course school, homework, and preparing for the SATs. It is a full-time job for my stepdaughter, Teri, to manage their calendars.

Since we moved to Arizona nine years ago, Bob

and I, too, have been on the go. Bob traveled back and forth to California every month on business for six years, remaining as a member of the board of directors for his former employer until 2006. His mom lived with us until her death in 2003. We both had major surgeries in 2004 and 2005. I started working at our church in 2005, first as a part-time bookstore clerk, then as human resources manager in 2006, and finally as the director of operations in 2008.

When Bob traveled, I would accompany him every month to visit my mom, help her with our family home, pay her bills, and of course, spend time with her in her last days. Cleaning out and selling our family homes filled our spare time. Oh, yes, and we also moved from one home into another. It was busy, and I thought at the time, out of balance.

Bob and I have been married fifteen years. He was the topic of my first book. As my second husband, he is my mulligan, or second chance. Not knowing specifically what I would write about in the book you are now reading, Bob asked, "You're not going to talk any more about me in your second book, are you?" Although his selfless nature towards me, his family, and friends would earn him eagle status, he is not necessarily among the eagles we will learn from in this book. He is the eagle, however, who taught me, among other things, to play golf and to understand a basic fundamental of the game, being in balance. Bob was an all-American golfer at Stanford. He cringes when I tell people that tidbit, and he responds by saying, "That was a hundred years ago." In reality, he attended Stanford in the late 1950s. So it was only fifty years ago!

In the early days of our relationship, when we were courting, he took me to a driving range in Montclair, California, to teach me to play. He bought me a set of clubs and helped me understand appropriate golf attire. On our first date to the range, I was wearing skin-tight pants. I must have been more concerned with looking good for my new beau rather than for what might be appropriate. Neither of us were Christians at the time. However, Bob, the consummate gentleman, politely suggested that perhaps I would feel more comfortable in a different pair of slacks. I had never been to a driving range and honestly didn't know what to expect. I thought the same attire for a miniature golf course would work on a driving range. Although Bob manufactured my swing from start to finish, my poor hand–eye coordination and klutziness made for abysmal swing results.

After our first range outing, I sported blisters on both hands from gripping the club too tightly. My toes were killing me by the end of the session. I couldn't wait to get out of those funky golf shoes. Golf shoes, back in the day, were kind of dorky looking. Mine were white with a huge flap covering the laces. If I had been a bird, I would most certainly have taken flight in a small gust of wind.

When I told Bob about my tender toes, he said, "You must not be in balance." I didn't understand what he meant. He explained I needed to keep my weight centered as I stood over the ball.[6]

At that time, golf didn't feel natural to me, but I wanted to enjoy it, as I knew how much Bob liked the game. For those of you who read *Mulligan*, this feeling cannot be compared with the grief I felt about having no interest whatsoever in my first husband's hobbies. In fact, playing in charity golf tournaments at that time was part of my job, so I wanted to learn as best I could. I did not want to embarrass myself,

---

6   If a golfer doesn't have his or her weight centered, or balanced, while addressing the ball prior to and while swinging the club, the ball's flight path may be to the left or right of its intended target—either the middle of the fairway or the green, dependent upon the golfer's current location.

Bob, or my employer; yet, I was a pretty sad case. Most of those golf outings were scramble formats[7], so I didn't end up playing that much, as my team rarely relied on any of my golf shots!

As the years pass, Bob continues to play. Now, at seventy-four and with debilitating arthritis, he finds it more and more difficult to muster any enthusiasm to play. Just before our upcoming vacation, Bob came home from playing a round of golf and announced he couldn't care less if he ever picked up a club again or not! I couldn't imagine this to be true. Golf has been part of his life for sixty-two years, as he started playing at age twelve. Instead of thinking how not playing any longer would adversely impact him, my thoughts, regrettably, were for me.

Yes, I just said that. Do you remember in the Introduction when I talked about wanting to write a book about things I felt you needed to hear? Well, there I was, once again centering my thoughts on my needs. If Bob didn't play golf, what would he want to do? Would it be something that would take

---

7 A scramble format is one in which there are four playing partners to a team. Each person will take alternate shots in the hope of using the best ball of the four to achieve par or less on a given hole for the team.

me away from what I wanted to do? Ugh. Yes, I just said that!

After I got over myself, the only thing I could think to say was, "Really?" I have learned after fifteen years of marriage that sometimes the best way to respond is to say nothing and let words simmer, soak in, and otherwise cook for a bit.

I was secretly hoping our upcoming vacation would give him pause to rethink his comment. He would give his clubs a rest and maybe have a change of heart. Was I hoping that change of heart would be for my benefit or his? In that moment I regrettably confess it was for the former.

On September 30, 2008, Bob and I left Sky Harbor Airport in Phoenix bound for San Francisco International Airport, referred to as SFO by California natives. Instead of writing during the short flight, I decided to listen to my iPod. I think it's interesting my favorite Christian group, Casting Crowns, started out in Daytona Beach, Florida, just a short drive from the home of Strang Communications. Hmm, probably just a coincidence?

Even before September 11, 2001, I was a white-knuckle flyer. I believe the root of my fear came from an article about a downed plane I read in early 2000. I recall with great clarity the way the writer expressed the fear that must have overwhelmed the flyers in the final fifteen seconds of their lives. I only wish I could write that well to make such an impact!

The writer wrote an in-depth biography about each of the deceased. That particular flight was headed back from Mexico, returning with happy and relaxed vacationers. The plane apparently dove deeply into a nose-first spin, pitching and rolling shortly after takeoff. This undoubtedly explains why takeoffs are hardest on me. After reading the article, I felt as if I knew each one of those poor people. The paper printed pictures of some of them while on their recent vacation. It was gloomy. It was macabre. It hit my soul. I never wanted to fly again. I didn't want to end up with someone reading about me in that way. That day I showed my fear to satan and his minions. Ever since, I have allowed him to capitalize on my weakness.

Our flight to SFO was especially bumpy, and per usual I was gripped in fear. I was surprised my palms didn't have blisters from gripping Bob's fore-arms, similar to the blisters I had from gripping the golf club so tightly the first time Bob took me to the driving range. I prayed to God for strength in the moment.

God gave me the opportunity to place my energy

elsewhere. I opened my backpack and brought out the composition notebook I purchased before we left on vacation so I could jot down some thoughts for this book. I honestly would have loved to bring my laptop with me, but in deference to my husband, who despises this piece of technology, I decided it best not to bring it along.

Unfortunately, I was too fearful to write. Needless to say, any thoughts I had for *Eagle* weren't taking flight. How could they, when I was in such a state of fear? Gosh, it sounds so ridiculous. After all, I am a child of God; whom shall I fear? According to my pastor, Lee McFarland, the words "do not be afraid" are referenced over 365 times in the Bible. Sounds like God gave us that reminder for each day of the year.

You may recall in the Introduction I wrote that I want to be an eagle. But, how could I be an eagle if, in the most literal sense, I couldn't bring myself to fly?

I then started to doubt if I would ever write this book. It was by the grace of God the first book came to pass. My love for Bob and God's grace in showing mercy on me were ideas readily committed to paper. Despite what I felt I wanted to say with this book, I didn't know if God was going to allow a follow-up book or books with the thoughts I was having, especially when I was allowing fear to dominate my thinking at that time. And what about my selfishness with Bob and his plight? In short, I tried to write, but couldn't.

I did have some random thoughts, however, about golf and living life for Christ. Suddenly, I had a burning desire to want to play golf—me, the self-proclaimed golf hack. You will recall in the introduction I wrote, "Stick me with a needle, poke a stick in my eye, but please, please don't ask me to spend four hours playing the game." What was happening?

After we arrived safely at SFO, I went through the same conversation I always have with Bob when we have just arrived somewhere safe via plane. The conversation typically recants my childish behavior and how I can't believe I allow satan and his minions to mess with my mind. I didn't tell him at the time about wanting to play golf; that declaration would come later.

Our plane for Hawaii wasn't leaving until the next day, so we enjoyed a nice dinner at a restaurant across the street from our airport hotel. We turned in around nine o'clock, and I awoke early the next morning convinced I was going to conquer my fear—or so I thought.

After getting through security, we immediately located a coffee shop to grab a quick bite before we went on to the gate to wait for our plane. I was excited about seeing our grandkids, yet honestly, here I was again starting to work myself up into a panic about the five-hour flight. While Bob sat calmly eating his cheese danish and sipping on his decaf white chocolate mocha, I pulled out my notebook, thinking I would write a few thoughts.

Unfortunately, I was still having trouble putting anything on paper. Maybe it was a case of writer's block, I thought. But what if a second book was just a fantasy and I was getting ahead of myself? Maybe I just needed to cool my heels, do my best to promote the first book, and let God do the rest.

We got to the gate and I started to sip on my own decaf white chocolate mocha. I was just about to pray for a smooth flight when a lady and her husband sat down next to us. She had beautiful long, sandy blonde hair and was dressed to the nines, complete with high heels and hose. I suddenly felt like a slob in my shorts, remembering my frumpy attire when we were in Allen's office at Strang.

Just as she and her husband were settling into their seats, situating their carry-on bags and wondering where they could get a cup of coffee, I interrupted their conversation and told them where the closest coffee shop was located. The older I get, the more I seem to insert myself into other people's lives—yikes!—a bad habit, to be sure. It's probably a good thing I don't have kids of my own.

Just then, the last words that a fearful flyer like me wants to hear were uttered by the gate agent. He was a small, bald-headed, beady-eyed man who announced with great clarity, and I quote, "Ladies and gentlemen, your plane to Hawaii has been delayed due to a mechanical problem. We are trying to avoid a worst-case scenario, so we hope you will be patient. I will get back to you as soon as I have more details."

What? I felt the blood drain from my face, my pulse began to skyrocket, and my palms were in an instant sweat. Bob sat calmly, like he didn't even hear this announcement. What was wrong with him? Why wasn't he joining me in panic?

The lady who had sent her husband off to the coffee shop said, "Hope our plane gets here soon. We are only in Hawaii for the weekend." I honestly don't remember what I said in response to her, but I mumbled something incoherent so as not to be rude. How was it possible that she wasn't afraid of the defective plane, either? How could she worry about only being there for the weekend? Even if we did get a plane that wasn't defective, we probably wouldn't make it at all! We would be one of those planes that would mysteriously go down in the Pacific—no survivors. I immediately tried to figure out our plane number to see if it sounded doomed. I know; it was pretty ridiculous!

"My husband works for the airlines," she said, "and we were given this opportunity at the last minute to go, so we of course said yes." *OK*, I thought, *here is someone who can get us a new plane!* Surely if her husband worked for the airline, he could make a call and have a new plane there in no time.

"My name is Nancy," she said. I think I introduced myself, but for a moment I didn't even know my own name.

And then, once again, as if out of a horror movie, that little beady-eyed man approached the sound system. I watched him carefully as he brought the microphone to his thin lips. In that moment, I don't think I knew of anything else that existed. "For those of you waiting here at the gate for your Hawaii flight, we are just trying to avoid a worst-case scenario"—*again with the worst-case scenario*—"and we are trying to get your plane here as soon as possible."

Did he not attend customer service training for the airlines? He must have missed the class on how to share information, especially with white-knucklers like me!

About that time, Steve, Nancy's husband, was returning with coffee in hand. She told him what was going on, and she introduced him to me. Again, I think I eked out a hello but totally forgot my manners and didn't introduce Bob. I can't believe I didn't introduce him to either one of them! My fear had me paralyzed. All I could think about was how Steve was going to save us. Steve?

Don't I have a Lord and Savior, whose name is not Steve?

What was wrong with me?

Steve sat down calmly next to Nancy. He proceeded to drink his coffee. He didn't strike me as a decaf white chocolate mocha guy, but more of an "I'll just have it black" kind of guy.

Although I wanted to jump out of my skin and immediately request he take action, I tried to collect myself. I meekly returned to my coffee. I felt my whole body become small and tense. Was no one listening to what was going on? Was I the only one that would take charge and do something? But what could I do?

I tried to get it together. *Jewelry,* I thought. *What? That is how I get it together?* I noticed a beautiful, stretchy gold ring on Nancy's finger. I had never seen anything like it before. I told her how stunning I thought it was. "I bought it for her while we were in Rome," Steve offered, "where I proposed." He told me of the catacombs and the cats in the catacombs and a bit more about their trip to Europe. For a minute I acted as if I could breathe and actually be civil.

Bob was still calmly reading. I finally collected myself long enough to introduce him to them.

I worked up the courage to ask Steve, "Do you think our plane will be OK?"

He said, "Sure, I am a mechanic for the airlines, and these guys know what they are doing."

I began to feel somewhat better about the situation. Meanwhile, Bob was still reading his book. *What drama is he reading that could possibly be any more harrowing than the one playing out right here?* I mused.

Then there he was again, the little gate agent. "For those of you waiting for the Hawaii plane, it appears as if the generator in the engine is causing the problem. It is not testing well." I looked at Steve as if he were an old friend. I was confident he could see the fear in my brown eyes. He said, "Let's hope they replace it rather than try to fix it. I am sure it will be fine."

Suddenly I was no longer feeling better about the situation.

Nancy, dear Nancy, must have seen the panic on my face, for in that moment she started telling me about where they would stay in Kona (if we ever made it). Bob and I had been there before, so I told her about how much fun she would have. Since their stay was to be short, I suggested she not feel as if she needed to see any other sights, because the hotel had everything. Her pleasant smile broadened when she offered, "I have heard you can swim with dolphins. I can't wait."

She then asked, "So, what do you do, Carolyn?" *Do?* I thought. *Me?* I didn't know anything in the moment. Could I admit to this total stranger that I was an active participant in the church? The obvious panic and fear in my voice and stiffened body parts made me totally ashamed to admit my leadership role in the church. Just then, I knew exactly how Peter felt when he denied Christ.

"Nancy," I said, "I am embarrassed in this moment to say I just finished working as a leader in Christian ministry."

"Why are you embarrassed?" she asked.

"Because," I admitted, "I shouldn't be so afraid of what is going on with our plane."

"That's all right, Carolyn. You're only human, and God understands."

I was ashamed to further tell her I had just written a book that honored God and marriage, but I did. Normally I would have happily shared that information, but in that moment, it was all I could do not to cry.

As she saw me holding back tears, she said, "I am a Christian. In fact, we both are, and it's OK, Carolyn."

Our plane finally arrived at the gate. I wasn't sure if it was a new plane or just one with a generator that passed its test, but I didn't seem to care. Steve and Nancy boarded the plane ahead of us and sat a couple of rows behind us. As Bob and I were getting settled into our seats, he said, "She seemed nice. She had really kind eyes." I responded, "You will never know how kind." I then started to tell him the drama that played out for me while he sat at the gate calmly reading his adventure book.

As I was unfolding the story, Nancy came over to see how I was doing. She didn't have to do that. If it were me and the roles had been reversed, I would have probably just told Bob about it and that would have been the end of it. Bob relinquished his seat to her so we could chat.

As she sat down, with the warmth of the sun shining through the airplane window, she looked as if she were surrounded by the light of God. I felt at peace with her.

"Nancy," I said, "God sent you to change the emphasis of the second book I am about to write." I told her my idea, and a smile came over her face. Her eyes lit up like those of a child on Christmas morning. We hugged. In that moment, I realized what an incredible blessing He had just sent—a stranger to encourage me in my faith, reveal my ridiculous fears, soften my heart to my shameful and selfish ways, and give us this story.

I had a lot to mull over on that flight. How long had my desire to do things I wanted affected Bob, members of my family, my friends, acquaintances, and even strangers? I thought back over the years and recalled the times that my life felt out of balance.

I realized in that moment that these times are given to us so we may grow in Him. He was giving me opportunities to be balanced in Him, yet I was too self-involved to realize what He was doing.

How long had my out-of-balance behavior, selfishness, and fear negatively impacted my relationship with and for Christ? The times Bob and I were doing things for others, namely our families, I had regarded them with contempt. Shame on me. My center at the time needed to be in Him, and clearly it wasn't.

I was overwhelmed. I started thinking about Bob's declaration that he no longer wanted to play golf and why I suddenly wanted to play. *He can't quit,* I thought. *He can't give up. Never in my life have I desired anything more than to begin to play the game. I want to keep it alive for him. I can't let him let go. Like a golfer gripping the club too tightly, yes, I sometimes grip him too tightly as well. I am still out of balance, fearful, and not trusting Him as I should.*

I was convinced, as we were well into cruising altitude, that God sent Nancy for a variety of reasons, none the least of which was to tell me how He wanted this story told. *Eagle* would indeed take flight, but He reminded me, it would be God-inspired and not Carolyn-inspired, just as the first book had been.

Bob looked at me with his usual understanding and smiled softly as if he knew what I was about to do. I told him everything that had happened from the time he told me he didn't want to play golf anymore to my time at the gate, Nancy's reassurance, *Eagle*'s new theme, and how I didn't want to lose him.

It was then I finally cried. I had been holding back tears since we were in Allen's office in Florida. While those would have been tears of joy, these were tears of shame. I pulled out my composition notebook and wrote, "I am without faith." I wrote everything that happened up to that point.

When we arrived at the Kona Airport, we saw Steve and Nancy at baggage claim. We exchanged e-mail addresses, and I thanked her again and told her I would send a copy of *Mulligan* so she could see if she wanted to associate herself with future writings. We hugged again and parted ways.

Bob and I headed for the rental car counter via shuttle bus. The rental car shuttle drivers in Kona seemed markedly different from those in Florida—much quieter and less entertaining. We rented a Lincoln Town Car, completely out of character for us. We would normally rent an econo-car, much like we did in Florida, but we thought the larger car would accommodate the family as we went around town. We dubbed it "the boat." The decision to rent it turned out to be a bit of a mistake. The parking spaces in downtown Kona are pretty small, and our son-in-law had already rented a minivan. We forgot about that little tidbit.

We got "the boat" and made our way to our rental condo. Fortunately, we didn't encounter any road tolls along the way as we had in Florida.

The condo was on the top floor of a three-story unit—three stories...hmm...just like the Strang building; another coincidence? It slept seven people, and it was ideal and relatively inexpensive.

Before settling into the condo, we decided to go to the grocery store to get some food and supplies. There we were again, worried about our next meal. Remember how we were in Florida? After we finished shopping, Bob said, "Let's go see what is playing at the movies in case the kids get bored and wanna see a movie."

What movie do you think was playing? *Eagle Eye.* Coincidence? I think not! My eyes must have been as big as saucers. I was practically yelling at Bob, "Look, look what is playing!" Yes, *Eagle* is completely and without a doubt His story.

When we got to the condo and unpacked, we sat outside on the deck and took a breath. Our deck overlooked the Pacific Ocean, the ocean I had been worried about the plane crashing into.

To the left of our condo sat the twelfth green of the local golf course. Palm trees served as the backdrop for the green. The thirteenth tee, following the twelfth green, was in our view as well. Next to it was a black lava blowhole.

To the right of the condo was the Kona coast, housing miles of black sandy beach with similar condos. It was truly a spectacular site, very calming and extremely picturesque. *Thank You, God, for such an awesome vacation spot,* I thought.

The deck was housed with two chaise lounges and a round table with chairs. Off to the side of the deck was a taller table with two higher stools. In addition to enjoying the view, Bob was finishing his novel, as he only had a few pages left, and I brought out my composition book. The kids weren't arriving for a couple of days, and I wanted to see if God wanted me to write.

I was thinking about how best to tell this story using golf metaphors. God had just given me the idea of balance; fundamental for success in golf and in Christ. But was that what He wanted for Chapter 1?

Just then, out of the corner of my eye, there he was. I spotted a young boy paddle-surfing. He was actually standing on a board in the middle of the ocean using an oar to paddle his way down the coastline. What incredible stamina and strength and, now, an incredible metaphor offered by God. The young man needed balance beyond compare to do what he was doing. He also needed sure footing. He was standing strong as he paddled.

So it is with those of us who long to be in balance with God, having a firm footing in our faith.

> If you do not stand firm in your faith,
> you will not stand at all.
> —Isaiah 7:9

As if my story with Nancy, the name of a movie, and a paddle surfer weren't enough to convince me to write this book, let me share one more "in-your-face" reminder from God applicable to this chapter.

When Bob and I went back into the condo after spending an hour or so out on the deck, we turned on the television to see what channels were available. What movie do you think was playing? It was an Alfred Hitchcock movie, a thriller made in 1958 called *Vertigo*. It starred Jimmy Stewart and Kim Novak. Jimmy Stewart's character, in moments of stress, suffered with a medical condition known as vertigo. This condition renders someone off-balance. *I got it, God!*

Thanks to Him, my Rock and Redeemer, for confirming this chapter's topic of balance and the importance of standing firm in our faith.

This story may sound truly incredible, but I was totally blown away at what God did next.

ॐ

Circle the answer to each question that best describes your life right now.

- Do you feel as if your life is out of balance? Yes / No

- If you answered yes, is it because you are not firmly balanced in Christ? Yes / No

- If you answered no, are you truly standing firm in your faith? Yes / No

If you answered yes to the first question and are not balanced in Christ, list a couple of ways you can make Him your center. (Ideas: daily prayer, modifying a weekend hobby to attend church or volunteer at church, spending more time with the people He gave you to love, or encouraging a stranger a day.)

_____

_____

_____

_____

The next question may be a bit harder to answer.

- Are you a natural encourager (i.e., Can you comfort a stranger if the opportunity presents itself, most especially when you have nothing to gain)? Yes / No

God gave me this acrostic for us to remember:

E — Encourage
A — And
G — Give
L — Love
E — Easily and Eagerly

For they refreshed my spirit and yours also. Such men deserve recognition.

—1 CORINTHIANS 16:18

If you have any encouragement from being united with Christ, if any comfort from his love, if any fellowship with the Spirit, if any tenderness and compassion, then make my joy complete by being like-minded, having the same love, being one in spirit and purpose.

—PHILIPPIANS 2:1–2

But encourage one another daily, as long as it is called Today, so that none of you may be hardened by sin's deceitfulness.

—HEBREWS 3:13

...Let us encourage one another— and all the more as you see the Day approaching.

—HEBREWS 10:25

Thanks to Nancy and those of you like her. You are greatly appreciated and loved!

For those of you out of balance, like me, take heart.

May our Lord Jesus Christ himself and
God our Father, who loved us and by
his grace gave us eternal encouragement
and good hope, encourage your hearts
and strengthen you in every good deed
and word.

—2 THESSALONIANS 2:16–17

 ᔓ

Before we head to Chapter 2, I want to share with
you that I am not presently attending postgraduate
school. After two months, I found it was consuming
eight to ten hours of my day; that is, if I wanted to
maintain my A- average. I was taking online classes
at home on my computer but never saw Bob! In
fact, we had gotten away from reading the Word,
something we are now back doing every day.

Faith, family, friends, and work—as long as faith
is first, we can remain in balance. The only way for
us to achieve balance in our lives is to have Christ
at our center. If we place our needs, our wants,
our desires at our center, we will surely lose our
footing.

chapter 2

FOCUS ON THE BALL

Keeping Our Eyes on Christ

W HILE BALANCE IS central for under-par results in golf, the second fundamental for any golfer is to keep one's eye on the ball.

I can't tell you the times I have topped[8] that silly little golf ball. I suppose I am anxious to see how far down the fairway the ball has traveled. I can't wait to see my results. Well, I don't have far to look when I have topped the ball, as it will probably be a good ten to twenty feet ahead of me. This is really embarrassing, especially when other people are watching.

Interestingly enough, as a Christian more often than not I find it difficult to focus my attention on

---

8   Topping the ball can occur when the golfer has taken his or her eye off of it at or before the club's impact with the ball. When this happens, the ball does not become airborne; in fact, it will skim the surface of the fairway.

Christ and what He did for us. My focus as of late has been bombarded with things of this world.

For example, my retirement nest egg has been badly broken. In fact, I would say it has been completely scrambled in this horrible economy. Every day I watch the news and listen to talk radio, and I see or hear about yet another politician playing with my livelihood and the future of our country. Christian pastors are being gunned down in the pulpit. Behaviors God told us He despised are being condoned in our tolerant culture. People are turning to phony-baloney religions for comfort. Our world is dominated with terrorists bent on our destruction, and as if this all were not enough to detract us, we hear of wars and rumors of wars.

Christ spoke about the End of the Age saying:

> For many will come in my name, claiming, "I am the Christ," and will deceive many. You will hear of wars and rumors of wars, but see to it that you are not alarmed. Such things must happen, but the end is still to come. Nation will rise against nation, and kingdom against kingdom. There will be famines and

earthquakes in various places. All these
are the beginning of birth pains.
                              —MATTHEW 24:5–8

OK, did you read anything in that scripture
about tsunamis? No, neither did I.

Bob and I were driving toward downtown Kona
on Alii Drive, the main drag. This two-lane highway
is butted right up against the Pacific Ocean. As the
kids would arrive the next day, we wanted to get
the lay of the land.

There it was, another sign. This time it was a
literal sign, a yellow-and-blue road sign. It read:

Entering Tsunami Evacuation Area

A black stick figure running toward a huge blue
tsunami-like wave accompanied the words on the
sign. Well, that certainly serves as a warm welcome
for visitors…*not!* All I could think was, *C'mon,
God, I am supposed to be on vacation!* Did I really
need one more thing to take my focus away from
Him and from my family? I couldn't believe my
eyes.

Bob was driving when we passed the sign, of
course. He wouldn't be caught dead with me behind

the wheel of a rental car! He figures we don't have enough insurance for the accident I would undoubtedly cause. Because he was paying attention to the road, he couldn't verify the sign at that moment. He even went so far as to question its existence. What? Did he think I made it up? Or better still, maybe he thought I couldn't read a road sign. If Alii Drive hadn't been a two-lane highway, I swear I would have insisted we turn back. Unfortunately, it was impossible to negotiate a U-turn with "the boat." I knew we would pass that dreaded sign again. I would be vindicated.

Was the State of Hawaii trying to pull a fast one? Apparently not. I suspect the sign was posted shortly after the horrific tsunami of 2004 in Indonesia. I am still chilled by the television images of people trying to climb palm trees to survive and of the floating bodies, or the thought of the disease and the lives lost in an instant. Again, much like the happy Mexican vacationers who died in the plane crash I spoke of in Chapter 1, entire coastal communities and over 225,000 people were gone in a matter of seconds.

So, there once again was that little brat known as satan trying to create in me more fear. *C'mon Carolyn, get a grip!*

"Who of you by worrying can add a
single hour to his life?"

—MATTHEW 6:27

"Where is your faith?" he asked his
disciples.

—LUKE 8:25

We made our way into downtown Kona and found
a parking lot with spaces that would accommodate
"the boat." We proceeded to do some window-shopping. All the while I was waiting for the alarm to
sound that the tsunami was on its way.

We happened upon a back alley and ventured
into its recesses. A small café stopped us in our
tracks. Yes, we were again in search of a meal! The
Three Birds was its name; no, not the Three Eagles,
but it was nonetheless appealing. Apparently, the
place is known for its homemade brownies. As both
of us are huge chocolate lovers, we couldn't resist.

We passed the historic royal palace and the first
Christian church in Hawaii, which date back to
the time of the early missionaries. I love learning
a locale's history. I marvel at how God has brought
His world together.

But once again, I found my focus going elsewhere

instead of enjoying the time with my hubby when I read a sign on the palace indicating it was undergoing renovations from a recent earthquake. Would it ever stop?

I decided I would just stop reading any and all signage.

> Immediately Jesus reached out his hand and caught him. "You of little faith," he said, "why did you doubt?"
>
> —MATTHEW 14:31

We determined the best thing to do to preserve my sanity was to return to the condo—the condo, of course, that stared at the Pacific Ocean, the ocean that was not to be crashed into by a plane but that would crash into our condo. Yikes!

We walked back to the car, all the while passing by happy shoppers, triathletes training for their race, locals speeding by on their mopeds, and kids playing on their boogey boards in the surf. They all seemed oblivious to the impending doom. They were all too busy focusing on what they were doing.

On the drive back to the condo, I tried to concentrate on something other than my fears. I started thinking about how much the islands had changed since Captain Cook discovered what he referred to as the Sandwich Islands in the late 1700s.

There are seven other islands that comprise the State of Hawaii: Kauai, Maui, Molokai, Lanai, Niihau, Oahu, and Kahoolawe. Each has its own beauty different from its sister islands, to be sure.

In the Hawaiian language, the word *kona* refers to the west side of something. Kona is located on the west side of the island of Hawaii, or "the Big Island," as it is referred to by the locals. God created Hawaii by raising it from volcanic activity. That must have been quite a show! Consequently, this island is not green and lush but is covered in black lava rock.

Hawaii County includes the Kona coast and is home to about 174,000 people.[9] Each October, Kona plays host to a triathlon, welcoming athletes from all over the world. They bike, swim, and run. Whew, it makes me tired just writing about the event.

My mind then wandered to another island in the chain I enjoyed visiting as a youngster, Kauai. Kauai

---

9 Information retrieved from CLRSearch.com, http://www.clrsearch.com/RSS/Demographics/HI/Kailua_Kona/Population_And_Growth (accessed April 17, 2009).

is the northernmost in the chain and gets a lot of rain. This rainfall makes it very lush, but the island has been home to devastating hurricanes. Remember Hurricane Iniki back in September 1992? *Ugh... Stop Carolyn...focus...beautiful vacation...awesome husband...soon to arrive grandkids...*

My thoughts then wandered to my father.

I suppose one of the reasons I enjoyed Kauai so much is because it is one of the few places my parents took me and my sister back in the early 1970s. I remember my mom making garments made from matching fabric for each of us to wear—a shirt for my dad and muumuus, or long Hawaiian dresses, for herself, my sister, and me. Yes, I know this sounds totally outrageous by today's cultural norms, but as a twelve-year-old kid, I thought it was the coolest. My mom was a great seamstress, so I was proud to wear what she made on her Singer sewing machine. The machine was black and gold. I can still see her turning the hand wheel and using a knee pedal to propel it into action. Amazing!

My family had been part of a tour group of other first-time visitors. Of course we were first-timers. With our colorful Hawaiian attire, we were the quintessential tourists!

We went to a pineapple plantation; took a boat

ride on the Fern Grotto, typically a location for weddings; and stopped at a mountain called the Sleeping Giant. I was fascinated by this formation. With my youthful and vivid imagination, I conjured up all kinds of thoughts of an actual sleeping giant.

Among the travelers on our tour bus were two women, a mother and her daughter, whose name was Anne Marie. Anne Marie was confined to a wheelchair and had severe physical and mental challenges. My father, my incredible father, offered to help the tour guide in hoisting her on and off the bus.

This was the first time in my short-lived existence that I understood the importance of focusing on others. Admittedly, I don't recall being able to show her or her mother grace. I wish I could tell you that I pitched in to help my father, but I honestly don't remember what I did.

In many ways the memories of those days seem far removed, yet I can still smell the first fragrant flower lei I ever wore and taste the purple paste called *poi* we ate at our first luau. Oh, yes, and who could forget the sight and smell of a pig being smoked in a six-foot-deep pit? This was a new sight for a youngster from California.

But most especially, I remember my father and his focus. He was on his vacation, yet he put his enjoyment aside, if even for a few moments, to help someone else. Although I grew up not knowing Christ and, quite honestly, don't know what my father knew of Christ at the time, it is clear that he recognized the importance of helping others.

> "The King will reply, 'I tell you the truth, whatever you did for one of the least of these brothers of mine, you did for me.'"
>
> —MATTHEW 25:40

Bob and I made it back to the condo sans tsunami alarms, and I asked if we could go play golf. I figured we might as well if we were going to be overtaken by a wave. I would try to get in eighteen holes, and maybe Bob could feel enjoyment in a different golf venue.

It was a beautiful, balmy, tropical afternoon. As you might have already guessed, I am a fair-weather golfer. I only like to play when it is about 85 degrees, no wind, and otherwise all conditions are perfect.

Bob said, "I will go as long as I don't have to play." So much for my "different venue" theory. Oh well, I figured that was a start. At least he agreed to still be out on the course.

We got back into "the boat" and started up the hill that would take us to the nearest public course. "Wait," I shouted suddenly. Bob slammed on the brakes. "What?" he responded.

There it was, a sign that read, Leaving the Tsunami Evacuation Area. Praise God, we were saved! Suddenly I had a new lease on life. I could play golf without any fears. I could completely focus on the game. Seriously, I know this sounds ridiculous, but in that moment I believed that we were out of danger, all because of a sign I read. Bob just smirked.

We got to the course and went into the pro shop. We signed up as a one-some and a rider. I really don't like to play with strangers, as I am a hack, remember? It is only fun when Bob and I play together.

We ate lunch at the golf course's restaurant over-looking the ocean. It was really quite lovely. And there we were once again eating.

I rented a set of clubs, as I hadn't packed mine from home. I never really expected to play while on vacation, what with Bob's declaration about not wanting to play, not to mention my previous aversion to playing.

I loved the feel of the rented clubs. They were so much lighter than my set, which was purchased in the 1990s. My clubs always felt as if I was lifting a pickax or a sledgehammer, though I might as well use those tools, the way I play. Actually, maybe they would work better!

We headed out to the first tee, and I was ready to play. I felt relaxed. I was able to focus on all the things Bob was instructing me to do. The course overlooked the ocean. I was still remarkably calm. Hey, we were out of the danger zone, right? I couldn't imagine how it was that we were above the evacuation area, insomuch as we still seemed close to the water. But oh well, if the sign said we were safe, then we must have been safe, right?

Lamentations 3:37–38 is a great reminder here: "Who can speak and have it happen if the Lord has not decreed it? Is it not from the mouth of the Most High that both calamities and good things come?"

These things don't come from a road sign, or a man named Steve. Egad…Remember how I thought Steve could save us from the worst-case scenario in Chapter 1?

Each of the holes on this golf course was fairly

straight, except for a few doglegs.[10] They were wide and generous fairways, a lot of room for a hack like me, or I hoped so, anyway.

I was enjoying the lessons Bob was giving on each hole, and he was having an element of fun also. My score after nine holes was sixty-nine. For my golfing readers, I would appreciate if you would stop laughing now. For my non-golfing readers, this is a *horrible* score. Most golf professionals will shoot this score for the entire eighteen holes. Thankfully, my ball was never once in any of the sand traps, and I was never out of bounds.

We were making our way around the course when we came to the seventeenth hole. The hole is a par three.[11] I placed my ball on the tee. This tee box was just above a ravine filled with black lava rock, beautiful flora, weeds, and who knows what little Hawaiian creatures.

I don't recall the club I used, maybe an eight iron. I kept my eye on the ball. I nailed it. I hit the ball squarely. It was actually airborne! Praise God! It ended up a few feet from the hole. I was jumping up

---

10 A doglegged hole bends to either the left or the right, from tee to green. Picture a dog's hind leg; you will then understand.

11 A par three means that it should only take three shots to get the ball into the hole.

and down, hooting and hollering, which is not very professional behavior for a golfer; but nevertheless, I was thrilled. We got back into our golf cart and followed the path to the green. I took my putter out of my bag, made my way toward my ball and was going to putt when Bob said, "Take it slow. Focus."

I stepped away from the ball. I asked Bob which way he thought the ball would break.[12] I took a deep breath and addressed the ball with my putter. I drew the club back in a slow motion away from the ball and exerted what I hoped was the correct amount of forward motion so that the ball would find the hole.

It did. I screamed. Bob had a huge grin on his sweet face glowing from the afternoon sun. There was a foursome just ahead of us on the next tee, and they turned to see what all the fuss was about. "I made it," I shouted.

Bob said, "Do you realize what you just did?"

"Yeah, I just got the ball into the hole," I replied.

"Yes, but you also just had a net eagle."

"What, what is that?" I asked.

---

12 The break refers to the direction the ball will go based on undulations in the green.

"Because of your high handicap.[13] instead of having a birdie or being one under par, you have what would be called a net eagle in tournament play."

Well, if that wasn't further in-my-face proof from God that He wanted me to write *Eagle,* I don't know what was. But He wasn't finished.

Up to that time, God had sent Nancy to show me this would be His book. He revealed a movie title with the word *eagle* in it just to move my thoughts along. Then He sent a paddle surfer to corroborate the golf metaphor of balance, along with another movie, *Vertigo,* just to make things interesting. Now for fun He put a cherry on top by allowing me to make an eagle.

That round of golf was my first in several years. Seriously, what were the odds? C'mon, even my fellow pessimists have to admit these coincidences were straight from Him.

Wow! It was almost too much!

Although I scored an eight on the last hole and ended up with a score of 124, I didn't care. I would hold on to that moment forever.

---

13 A handicap is when a better player will allow players of less ability the opportunity to level the playing field and give the lesser player a certain number of strokes.

The next day was Friday. We drove back through the evacuation area to pick up the kids from the airport. As I mentioned earlier, they rented a minivan, so we traveled in that wherever we went, leaving "the boat" behind at the condo.

It was a grand reunion. We greeted them with flower leis, just as I remembered being greeted long ago with my family in Kauai. We spent the rest of that day and Saturday getting settled in and went out to a nice dinner Saturday night. The place where we ate was right on the water, an open-air restaurant. The beach was a stone's throw from our table. We had the waiter take a picture of us. (You can see it in the back of this book.) Surrounded by my family, I don't recall being afraid of anything in that moment. As it was when I had the net eagle, I felt great joy.

> LORD, you have assigned me my portion and my cup; you have made my lot secure. The boundary lines have fallen for me in pleasant places; surely I have a delightful inheritance.
>
> —PSALM 16:5–6

On our way to the restaurant, I mentioned to the family that Bob and I were going to church in the morning, and they were more than welcome to join us. I noticed a quaint and extremely picturesque church situated on Alii Drive that first day we went window-shopping. I thought it was a Christian church, but as we passed fairly quickly, I didn't get a good look. I asked my granddaughter, who is great at spotting such details, if she could look for the name and the service times as we passed by on our way to the restaurant. As we came upon the church, she said, "It says Living Stones Church, and it looks like they have 7:30, 9:00, and 11:00 a.m. services."

Bob and I agreed that the 9:00 a.m. service was the best time to attend. That next morning, Bob and I left around 8:15 for church. We both wore Hawaiian attire. No, nothing with matching fabric, but as the church sat adjacent to a white sandy beach, we thought "aloha attire," as the locals call it, would probably be appropriate. Bob donned a yellow Hawaiian shirt covered in white hibiscus, accompanied by a pair of brown shorts. It is one of my favorite outfits on him. I wore a light blue spaghetti-strapped sundress dotted with black and orange flowers. I think I am rapidly reaching the age at which I really shouldn't be wearing dresses with spaghetti straps, but there I was. I also wore sandals and took a sweater.

We are so used to wearing what we want at our home church that, in all honesty, it would be a challenge to dress up. A coat and tie for Bob, and a dress with stockings and high heels for me—it's probably not going to happen. I talked a little bit about my and Bob's desire for casualness in worship in *Mulligan*. It's just my opinion, but I think we can still worship God eagerly, regardless of what we wear.

We arrived at Living Stones around 8:40 a.m. There were few marked parking spaces in front of the church. If someone hadn't been coming out just as we were coming in, we would have had to walk a good distance, and that is if we could have found parking at all on Alii Drive. Parking is at a premium, as homeowners along the street park their own cars on the road in front of their houses. Thanks to God, He got us a spot right in front!

According to Living Stones's pastor, Bill Barley, the building was constructed by Congregational missionaries in 1855 but was eventually abandoned in the mid-twentieth century. Because of the abandonment of use, title to the property reverted to the

State of Hawaii. Living Stones occupies the property under a lease from the state.

It is an amazing and historic stone structure. It sits on a patch of ground that juts out ever so slightly into the Pacific. As we walked up a short path to the entrance, on our right, we passed a couple of E-Z UP tents. One housed a few Christian books and general church information, the other had refreshments. I think I spotted some pineapple and grapes—after all, we are always on the hunt for sustenance. There may even have been several slices of banana bread also. It looked to me as if they were also serving up Kona coffee. *How cool,* I thought, since that was similar to our church, Radiant.

My first impression of this church was its charming Old World feel. I immediately started to draw unfair comparisons between it and Radiant.

As you know, we call Radiant Church our home. It is a mega-church that sits smack-dab in the middle of Surprise. The town, of course, is no longer a surprise to anyone, as our population is now over one hundred thousand. Situated in the desert, our church hosts between five thousand and six thousand each weekend. We have a killer sound system used by an awesome rock-and-roll worship team. We use multimedia presentations to welcome guests and videos to illustrate sermon points. We have Krispy Kreme donuts for everyone, a full bookstore housing tons of Bibles and Christian reading, along with the latest in Christian bling. We also have a full coffee shop and café. We even have our own Christian preschool. Of course, our pastor, Lee McFarland, is a riot, a Bible scholar, and a laid-back guy.

As it turns out, he is just like Pastor Bill from Living Stones. From the outside, we wouldn't have expected any of that from the quaint Hawaiian church, and quite frankly, we wouldn't have cared if they didn't have those things. We were up for a new experience and obviously didn't have a clue before we drove up as to what we were getting ourselves into. Our only requirement for the church was that it was Christian.

We walked a little further up the path to the sanctuary and were greeted by two freestanding flat-screen TVs projecting Pastor Bill's image. Wow, talk about twenty-first century meets nineteenth century. It was an incredible blend of nature and technology. The ocean was a stone's throw away, and there we were watching Pastor Bill in full color, waiting for the first service to let out while seated on a stone wall built by missionaries. The wall was obviously built to keep the waves from coming right into the church. That's how close the building is to the ocean.

Just behind the church, the kids were learning about God. There was an inflatable bouncy house for playtime and an E-Z UP where the kids were gathered under in worship—totally something we would do at Radiant, just not in the dead of our Arizona summer!

I felt so blessed in that moment that God would allow us to see that type of worship. It was different from our church home in terms of the ambiance but so similar in terms of the power of God, which permeated every stone, every blade of grass, and every wave that crashed against the wall. All this beauty He created outside. In our wildest dreams we couldn't have begun to imagine what He had in store for us inside.

We weren't waiting long before the first service let out. Bob and I are typically the first ones in attendance wherever we go. He hates to be late, so consequently we are always early.

As the people streamed down the few steps and made their way toward the banana bread—maybe it was macadamia nut bread; either way, I wish I would have tried some because it looked so yummy—we made our way inside. We were given a bulletin, and on its front were the words *Sunday Celebration.*

The seating capacity inside the church I would guess to be no more than one hundred. There were four sections of folding chairs. We found two that looked as if they had our names on them. They were in the last row in the middle section. We were lulled into relaxation by easy listening Christian rock music emanating from their sound system in a small corner of the back of the church. I took a moment to read the bulletin. On the inside front cover I found details of Sunday service times and their upcoming weekly activities. There were Bible classes, a high school ministry called Ignite, and a Bible-based stretch class called Yielding Ourselves to God's Authority, or Y.O.G.A. How cool is that? They have an outreach ministry and fellowship for eighteen year olds to thirtysomethings called 7:37. A seminar for Christian business owners and a women's retreat rounded out the upcoming activities. This church completely understands the importance of keeping God's people focused on Him at all times, just like Pastor Lee and the awesome Radiant team.[14]

I was humming along with the Christian music playing over a welcome video that gave more info on their prayer ministry, children's ministry, and

14 The Living Stones Church Web site is www.livingstones.us.

upcoming activities. They had a sermon slide asking visitors to turn off their cell phones. I smiled, as I could recall seeing Radiant's same slide.

There were four fans attached to the ceiling's corners. They were pointed directly over the four sections of chairs. This was awesome, as the doors remained open during the entire service. With the elevated humidity, the fans were most welcome. I was still reading the back of the bulletin, which detailed the importance of the gospel, when from my peripheral vision I noticed a woman walking to the front of the church. She began taking Communion bread out of a Ziploc baggie and distributing it among wicker baskets. I only noticed one cup and guessed that Communion there was done by intinction.

The worship leader went to the front carrying what looked like a guitar similar to what Radiant's worship leader uses. Another gentleman was holding a different type of guitar, and a drummer and backup vocalist rounded out the team. The worship leader was wearing jeans, praise God. We felt at home.

By this time the building was almost full. The worship leader asked us to rise and join him in song. This was, again, something we do at Radiant, and of course Bob and I did so with great joy. The idea of standing to praise our God is for us a no-brainer.

Are you ready for what came next? As he started
to play his guitar and the other members of his
team joined in, it happened. He started to sing "The
Everlasting God."[15] Here are the words:

Strength will rise as we wait upon the Lord
We will wait upon the Lord
We will wait upon the Lord

Our God, You reign forever
Our hope, our Strong Deliverer
You are the everlasting God
The everlasting God
You do not faint
You won't grow weary

Our God, You reign forever
Our hope, our Strong Deliverer
You are the everlasting God
The everlasting God
You do not faint
You won't grow weary

You're the defender of the weak
You comfort those in need
You lift us up on wings like eagles

Are you kidding me, God? was all I could think. This was to be the first worship song we sang? Was this another coincidence? No way.

I turned to Bob as we sang, and the tears came streaming down my face. It was a good thing we were standing in back. I sang that day like I had never sung to God before. As if all of the other promptings He sent weren't enough, this was the proverbial icing on the cake.

I honestly don't recall the other worship songs we sang. All I could think about was Him and His awesome might.

As we finished singing, a man in jeans and what looked to me like a blue Tommy Bahama aloha shirt came to the front. Just as I was imagining which of Pastor Lee's famous aloha shirts he was wearing back in Arizona, the man in the front introduced himself as Pastor Bill Barley. He offered his welcome and asked us to greet each other before we were seated.

I would guess Pastor Bill to be in his thirties. (Boy, I hope I am right! Forgive me, pastor, if you are younger than that.) He was very articulate as he made the announcements for the church. He mentioned a time of fellowship for women, an upcoming tea in the countryside. I wish I could have stayed for that event. Can you imagine what an awesome experience it must have been to have tea in the Hawaiian countryside in fellowship with other women of faith?

Before Pastor Bill preached, he said we would have Communion. He talked about its importance in the context of spiritual warfare. He quoted 1 Corinthians 11:23–26:

> For I received from the Lord what I also passed on to you: The Lord Jesus, on the night he was betrayed, took bread, and when he had given thanks, he broke it and said, "This is my body, which is for you; do this in remembrance of me." In the same way, after supper he took the cup, saying, "This cup is the new covenant in my blood; do this, whenever you drink it, in remembrance of me." For whenever you eat this bread and drink this cup, you proclaim the Lord's death until he comes.

He then invited us to come forward. I wasn't sure Bob knew what to do, as I don't think he had taken Communion by intinction before. He watched and learned. I just hoped my bread wouldn't fall into the cup.

As I approached Pastor Bill, I had tears streaming down my face. I can't imagine what he must have thought. As a pastor, though, I am certain he had seen this reaction before. We returned to our seats, and I sat and prayed, first a prayer of thanksgiving and then a prayer of commitment to write *Eagle*.

When Communion was finished, Pastor Bill began his sermon. His sermon title was "Faith over Fear."

Well, God certainly knew how to culminate a teaching for me. Let's see, through that trip alone, I had been faced with my fear of losing Bob, of flying, earthquakes, hurricanes, and tsunamis. Of course, all the other fears I mentioned earlier in this chapter I could heap on top of those. Pastor Bill could have used me for a great example of fear.

I didn't write down his sermon verbatim, but I tried to write down the scripture passages so I could reference them later. One of the references was Isaiah 41:10: "So do not fear, for I am with you; do not be dismayed, for I am your God. I will strengthen you and help you; I will uphold you with my righteous right hand." Another verse was from 2 Timothy 1:7: "For God did not give us a spirit of timidity, but a spirit of power, of love and of self-discipline." He also talked about Peter and the rooster crowing, a reference I used in the Preface.

The gist of his sermon emphasized saying no to fear and yes to faith. Several things he said struck a chord with me. He said, "We need to have faith and not fear for what we don't want to happen. God wants to use us at our point of greatest weakness. That is also what the enemy senses and wants to use."

Boy, have I been allowing the enemy to have his way. I don't want that anymore. Please, God, help me, I prayed.

After the service was over, it was all I could do to get to the car before breaking down in shame. God was not only sending me a message about this book, but He was also telling me to get a grip and not be so afraid. I sincerely want God to use my weakness, not satan.

My deepest and most profound thanks to Pastor Bill Barley for being such an awesome eagle for God, just like my pastor, Lee McFarland.

As an aside, when we arrived home, I sent an e-mail to Pastor Bill thanking him but also letting him know I was hoping to write about his church in this book. I told him I would send him a copy of

Mulligan, which included an excerpt from *Eagle,* so he could familiarize himself with my writing and determine, like Nancy, if he wanted to associate himself with me and my work for God.

A few weeks after I sent Pastor Bill the book, I received an e-mail from him saying, "Well done. Living Stones would be happy to be part of any future writings."

I didn't hear from him until a few months later, when he was asking the friends and family of Living Stones to pray for his wife, who was experiencing a severe health challenge. He opened his e-mail with the following scripture:

> Be joyful in hope, patient in affliction, faithful in prayer.
>
> —ROMANS 12:12

By the way, are you ready for yet another "coincidence"? Pastor Bill's hometown is Lake Mary, Florida, home of my publisher, Strang Communications!

ↄ

Here are a couple of questions for you, inspired by Pastor Bill's sermon. They are questions that will help build your flight pattern for God.

- Am I using my faith for what I don't want to happen? Yes / No

- If not, how will I commit to overcoming my fears?

_____

_____

_____

_____

As an aside, I pray that each day you offer thanks for your pastor and his staff. I have seen firsthand how diligently and tirelessly these people work for God. Their work does not just take place on Sundays. As a matter of fact, the team at Radiant Church only has one day off during the week, as we have service on Saturday night, too. Pastor Lee is the first one there and usually the last to leave. Even when he does leave the church, it is usually to go to a hospital visit or to perform premarital counseling for couples. He and his staff, as well as Pastor Bill and his staff, have given their lives to do God's work.

How often do you send notes of encouragement or thanks to your pastor and church staff? They don't expect it, but they would certainly appreciate the encouragement. They, more than any of us, are in a constant spiritual battle on our behalf.

They are a rare breed of eagles, to be sure. Please pray for their safety, good health, and strength to carry on against satan and his minions.

ↄ

God sent me an acrostic using a golf metaphor to help encourage me to overcome my fears. As I close this chapter, I will include it. Maybe it was for you, too.

Stop being a bogey! Remember, a bogey is when a golfer takes one too many shots on any given golf hole, causing him or her to be over par.

B — Being out of focus with Christ
O — Only
G — Gives
E — Evil a
Y — Yes

> Do not gloat over me, my enemy! Though I have fallen, I will rise. Though I sit in darkness, the LORD will be my light.
> —MICAH 7:8

In Acts 27:23–26, Paul said, "Last night an angel of the God whose I am and whom I serve stood beside me and said, 'Do not be afraid, Paul. You must stand trial before Caesar; and God has graciously given you the lives of all who sail with you.' So keep up your courage, men, for I have faith in God that it will happen just as he told me.'"

Jesus told his disciples in John 16:33, "I have told you these things, so that in me you may have peace. In this world you will have trouble. But take heart! I have overcome the world."

ご

Thanks to God, Bob has reset his focus and is back out on the golf course hopeful at some point this year to shoot his age, or a 74.

chapter 3

LINING UP TO THE TARGET
Aiming for Jesus

I T WAS THE last full day of vacation, and our
grandkids wanted to go to the beach. We had
just gone to a snorkeling beach the day prior,
and I hoped I would have the stamina to keep up.
At the snorkeling beach, we swam with some sea
turtles, ate sno-cones (I think my favorite flavor was
a combination of bubble gum and cotton candy),
munched on nachos, and scarfed down chili dogs. I
swam with a kind of abandon I had long forgotten.
I ate with such voracity I didn't care if my stomach
was bulging in my wetsuit or not. I couldn't believe
they wanted to head back for more so soon, but
that's a kid for ya, thanks be to God.

I would never have imagined that a day at the
beach would provide me with the third chapter of

this book. Although, from the way God had revealed things so far, I shouldn't have been amazed.

If you have ever been to the beach, you would probably agree that it is quite a different experience for adults than it is for children. My stepdaughter, Teri, who doesn't know a stranger, spent the majority of her time in the water chatting with a retired hotel employee learning everything about his life, his children's school, and the best local restaurants. My granddaughter, Stacy, now in her late twenties, and I decided to soak up our last few hours sunning ourselves and reading. She, a much better multitasker than I, was able to listen to her iPod while reading. My son-in-law, Terry, spent his day playing with our grandsons, although, unlike the boys, who are like Energizer bunnies, he joined Stacy and me at brief intervals to dry off and rest.

A day at the beach for my grandsons, Cameron and Austin, means bodysurfing and playing catch on the beach, either with each other or their dad. Both boys have fair complexions, so Teri ensures they are always adequately coated with sunscreen. Left to either of themselves, they probably couldn't care less about applying it.

Cameron, now seventeen, is fast approaching manhood. His youthful exuberance is giving way to more adult pursuits, like studying for the SATs, working toward his own share of eagles as a member of the Lodi High golf team, considering future vocations, and of course, girls!

My youngest grandson, Austin, now fourteen, is in the enviable and perhaps final stage of kid-dom. Austin can play basketball or baseball long after others have grown tired. Among his favorite foods are cheese pizza, popsicles, nachos, Pop-Tarts, and ice cream. He, of course, never gains an ounce. He could easily make a meal out of candy—any candy. He loves to play video games. He enjoys cartoons and family sitcoms, and he absolutely loves Christmas morning. I still have to wrap the packages in such a way that he can't figure out the contents, and he loves to play board games. On this vacation, he was the instigator of a familiar favorite, Yahtzee. We dubbed him the Yahtzee champ, although Cameron gave him a run for his money any number of times.

My primary activity on the beach was reading *War and Peace*. I am still reading it. Forgive me, Mr. Tolstoy, but your book is like a mouthful of Grape-Nuts; it just goes on and on. Anyway, I was sitting there thinking, *Gosh, I really don't care much for the sand in my toes, and boy, it sure is getting hot.* Most of the people on the beach that day were young families or young teen boys. Those boys were taking on the surf in what I thought was an aggressive manner. I was worried about the little kids and hoped their parents were watching them closely.

I went back to reading my book, the part where a young princess in the midst of childbirth is just about to die, when I gazed up over my book and noticed a young boy and the woman with him, who I assumed was his mom. This young boy was absolutely mesmerized by the ocean. He stared and stared at it for the longest time. His mom, noticing his fascination, turned to him and smiled. I turned to my granddaughter and told her, "Oh my goodness, I know the topic of the third chapter in my book." My eyes started to well with tears, and she said, "Oh, don't cry."

Then a little girl who couldn't have been more than three years old came up to her father and said, "Daddy, will you take me to swim in the water?" She was as cute as a button in her little pink one-piece swimsuit with the ruffles on her bottom. She had donned the tiniest of sunhats and sunglasses shaped like stars. Her father willingly obliged her request. When they returned just a few minutes later, she said, "Daddy, I love you," and then she proceeded to make a sand castle.

How God must long to hear those words from each of us.

Do you think any of those kids were, like I was, worried about getting sand in their toes? Do you think any adult would spend any amount of time, serious time, just looking at the ocean? Do you think any of those kids would choose to read *War and Peace* when the waves are beckoning them to dive in headfirst? Do you think any of those kids were worried about their safety or the safety of the people around them? Do you think they cared a hoot about a tsunami, a hurricane, or their parents' dwindling portfolios? The answer to all these questions most certainly is no.

Now, for my adult readers who still consider themselves to be like kids, able to play charades or board games with other couples or friends—that's great. However, your pleasure is probably short-lived, a brief respite from your adult responsibilities.

Watching these children, my grandsons included, made me realize why Jesus said what He said about children and why He was so concerned with them coming to Him.

> But Jesus called the children to him
> and said, "Let the little children come
> to me, and do not hinder them, for the
> kingdom of God belongs to such as
> these. I tell you the truth, anyone who
> will not receive the kingdom of God like
> a little child will never enter it."
>
> —LUKE 18:16–17

What does that scripture mean for those of us adults wishing to soar for Him? Is it too late, even for those of us born again in Him? Of course not, but it does mean, I think, that our approach to a life in Him means we have to aim for Him. As a golfer aligns his or herself with the target, namely, the golf hole located on the green, we as Christians must not only take care to align ourselves with Him, but we also must see that our children are aimed at Him, too.

In the Luke passage above, Jesus scolded the disciples when they thought that the people who were bringing their babies to Him for a blessing were a bother. I am not a Bible scholar, nor do I profess to be, but it seems to me that Jesus recognized the importance of children to the kingdom for a myriad of reasons.

First, in Paul's first letter to the Corinthians he says, "In regard to evil be infants, but in your thinking be adults" (1 Cor. 14:20). Children don't know evil until they start to mature, and either learn it from their friends or our culture. In the worst of cases, they learn it from those closest to them.

Second, Psalm 78:1–4 proclaims, "O my people, hear my teaching; listen to the words of my mouth, I will open my mouth in parables, I will utter hidden things, things from of old—what we have heard and known, what our fathers have told us. We will not hide them from their children; we will tell the next generation." The psalmist, Asaph, knew the importance of sharing God and His glory with future generations.

Third, King Solomon offered this in Psalm 127:3: "Sons are a heritage from the LORD, children a reward from him." The memories with my grand-children on this vacation and at other times are precious, to be certain. Other children in my life who are equally as dear are my sister's children. I remember as if it were just yesterday time I spent long ago with my oldest niece, now thirty, playing with She-Ra and Cabbage Patch dolls; with my nephew, now twenty-seven, at his pinewood derby, a Cub scout event; and letting my youngest niece, now eighteen, paint my fingernails when she was three or four. I played babysitter to my best girl-friend's daughter in her younger years, too. Our favorite breakfasts were chocolate-flavored Slim Fast, and our dinners were usually popcorn and Twinkies!

Fourth, Jesus acknowledged the importance of children in Mark 9:36–37, 42.

> He took a little child and had him stand among them. Taking him in his arms, he said to them, "Whoever welcomes one of these little children in my name welcomes me; and whoever welcomes me does not welcome me but the one who sent me....And if anyone causes one of these little ones who believe in me to sin, it would be better for him to be thrown into the sea with a large mill-stone tied around his neck."

Finally, Paul wrote:

> But as for you, continue in what you have learned and have become convinced of,

because you know those from whom you learned it, and how from infancy you have known the holy Scriptures, which are able to make you wise for salvation through faith in Christ Jesus. All Scripture is God-breathed and is useful for teaching, rebuking, correcting and training in righteousness, so that the man of God may be thoroughly equipped for every good work.

—2 Timothy 3:14–17

At Radiant Church, Pastor Lee places the highest emphasis on our children's and youth ministry. He realizes in our pop culture the importance of making church interesting for kids. If it is interesting for kids, then the parents will follow, if they aren't already with us.

If we wish to be eagles, we must align ourselves with Him as a child would. He wants us to be excited to be with Him, as excited as Austin is opening packages on Christmas morning, or for my golfing readers, as excited as Phil Mickelson was when he jumped a whopping two feet off the ground the year he finally won the Masters!

God wants desperately to hear those words: "I love you, Daddy."

Of course, as adults we naturally take on grown-up responsibilities, we take care of ourselves and those around us, we grow our faith, and we learn to discern. As Paul said in 1 Corinthians 13:11, "When I was a child, I talked like a child, I thought like a child, I reasoned like a child. When I became a man, I put childish ways behind me." But putting behind us childish ways shouldn't include forsaking our exuberance—especially not our exuberance for living a life in Him. Forgetting our childish ways doesn't include forgetting about the purity found in loving those around us. Leaving our childish ways should never mean turning our backs on our natural inclination to gravitate toward Him.

As I end this chapter, I am reminded of a childhood memory. We lived in a small unincorporated area in northern California called El Sobrante, which, in Spanish, means "remainder." It's on the outskirts of the San Francisco Bay area. Our house was on a small dead-end street, and we knew all our neighbors. This was the only home I ever knew as a child. The neighbor kids and I played baseball, kick the can, and hide-and-go-seek in the street.

My dad was a weekend golfer. He played about

as much as I do today, which is, as you know, hardly at all. All I remember of his equipment was a brown leather golf bag. I couldn't have been more than seven when I took a golf ball out of that bag. I proceeded to take the ball out to the sidewalk in front of our home. I wanted to see what was inside the ball. I rubbed and rubbed that ball on the sidewalk for hours on end. I was very persistent. I don't know how long it took me to get past the dimpled white exterior, but I finally made it to the heart of the ball. It looked like a wadded ball of string. To this day, I can still smell the rubber on the inside.

It occurs to me that God had already gotten past our dimpled exterior when He sent His Son to die on a cross for us. It is the rubber, or whatever material golf balls are made of today, that gives the ball flight. He wants our lives in Him to take flight. But we can only do that if we can receive Him with our inner material, or our inner child.

King Solomon said, "Even a child is known by his actions, by whether his conduct is pure and right" (Prov. 20:11). Solomon, and of course, Jesus, knew that a person's character is formulated as a child. Parents, please help align your children with Him. He is their target. He is your target. Just as you desire to be under par in Him, they do, too; but they need you to guide them.

Finally, a suggestion for us adults: My grandson Austin loves to swim. He also loves to practice all sorts of jumps into the pool, and he names his jumps—like the Chunky Monkey or the SpongeBob Splash. Let's join God in the deep end of the pool. Next time you are swimming with your kids at the local pool or at the beach, do a cannonball for God and call it the Lord's Leap!

> The blind and the lame came to him at the temple, and he healed them. But when the chief priests and the teachers of the law saw the wonderful things he did and the children shouting in the temple area, "Hosanna to the Son of David," they were indignant. "Do you hear what these children are saying?" they asked him. "Yes," replied Jesus, "have you never read, "'From the lips of children and infants you have ordained praise'"?
>
> —MATTHEW 21:14–16

ॐ

Answer the questions below:

- Are you and your family aligned with a Bible-based church? Yes / No

- Have you had your child dedicated to Him? Yes / No

- Have you encouraged your child in a relationship with Christ? Yes / No

- In the last twenty-four hours, have you told your child you love him or her? Yes / No

- In the last twenty-four hours, have you played a game with your child? Yes / No

If you answered no to any of the questions above, my only remaining question is, why not? My prayer is that you will always and in every way honor the children in your life.

﹋

God's acrostic for this chapter reminds us to remember Him, since we are His children.

G — God
O — Our
L — Loving
F — Father

chapter 4

THE FINISHING HOLE

WHEN I FINISHED writing this book's first chapter, I asked Bob if he would read it and give me his thoughts. He is my best critic, not to mention a great editor. He walked into my home office after reading it and had a perplexed look on his face. Our dog, Pookie, an eighteen-pound poodle-Yorkie mix followed closely behind him. She wasn't in her usual trot but was walking about as slowly as he. Both had hang-dog countenances to be certain.

Oh dear, I thought. *This can't be good.*

He said, "I don't want you to feel hurt by what I am going to say, OK? But, do you really think anyone will care a hoot about our vacation?" he asked. He quickly followed it up with, "I do think your writing has improved a lot since *Mulligan,* though."

I wondered which of the two, the question or

the statement, he thought would be less hurtful. I know he was being honest and helpful; that is why I asked for his opinion. However, I wasn't expecting that sort of response at all. I told him on the plane the direction *Eagle* was headed, so it's not like he didn't know where I was going with the story. In fact, he was right there with me as all of the signs unfolded. Yet, now that I think of it, at the time he never agreed or disagreed that it was a story he felt needed telling.

"Please don't stop writing," he added. "Finish the book and then we can revisit it." I agreed that the best thing to do was to get the book written. We would then read it through and see if it was a story worthy of publishing.

So, I shut down my computer for the evening. I went into the kitchen to see if I could locate some comfort food but couldn't find anything to satisfy. Bob gave me a hug and kiss and tried his best to console me. He went on for a bit about why he didn't want me to stop writing. Admittedly, I felt as if some wind had been taken out of my sails, particularly when I felt as if God had been speaking right to me for two solid weeks and since I committed to Him at Living Stones that day that I would write.

I went into our family room and sat down

to watch television. My sweet little dog, Pookie, cuddled up next to me as if to say, "It's OK, Mommy," and then she proceeded to fall asleep. As the TV guide was coming into my view, I went to the movie channels. No, *Eagle Eye* wasn't playing this time. However, one of my favorite movies was playing, *National Treasure: Book of Secrets.* This is the second one in the series and probably the better of the two.

As Bob and I were chatting earlier, I didn't realize the movie was on or I would have tuned in sooner. Before I chose the movie from the guide, I realized it was about three-quarters over. I thought, *I might as well go to bed,* but then changed my mind, as I am prone to do. Besides, I wasn't really tired and wanted to see that beautiful city of gold.

Well, I tuned in just in time to see Nicolas Cage and his fellow treasure-seekers standing high atop the Black Hills in South Dakota at Mt. Rushmore. They were pouring bottled water all over the rock to try and locate the symbol that would reveal the final clue that would lead them to a golden city. They finally found it! They referred to it as the "powerful bird," the "warrior." Yes, it was an image of an eagle.

This was my final sign from God. I would not be deterred. His story would be told.

Perhaps my husband is right and you couldn't care less about what happened to me on vacation. But think about times when you had an experience and thought, "Is this from God?" Truly, I believe that He sends us experiences to strengthen our relationship with Him.

From the time God gave me the idea for *Mulligan* to that final moment watching *National Treasure*, I realized the power of God in all the details of our lives. He is ever present if we just look for Him; whether it is while we work, in our daily interactions, in the game of golf, or while on vacation.

He never leaves us. He wants to be our balance and to be in our focus. He wants us to be eagles and fly easily, aligning our flight pattern with His.

☙

As I close, I offer one final story that has nothing to do with a movie, a road sign, or an eagle. It is an e-mail from a friend.

I hadn't heard from another friend of mine for months until just as I was finishing this book. Out of the blue, our mutual friend asked if she could

pass on my e-mail address to the friend with whom
I had lost contact. She said I had been on her mind
a lot lately. Naturally, I gave the address to our
mutual friend, and here is what I received.

Hi there, my friend!

I hope and pray that you and Bob are
doing well and are healthy and happy. I
have missed you so much and have been
thinking about you so much lately. I
am so curious about the progress of the
book. Is it out in stores yet? If so, how is
everything going? What amazing things
is God doing through your book and
your life since it came out? I just cannot
wait to hear the testimonies of how He
is using it to bless His kingdom and His
people!

I'm so sorry that I did not get a chance
to talk to you before I left. I have to tell
you the story.

We opened our store on November 1,
and *my* plans were that within a month,
maybe two, we would be able to hire a
full-time manager to work the majority
of the hours and my husband and I

would fill in the gaps. Well, by December it was already very clear to me that was not going to happen because we were not selling enough to even pay the overhead without labor. I had planned to work Saturday and Sunday and keep up all my other responsibilities and volunteer activities, and within that first month I was backsliding big time. I was getting up on Sunday mornings saying, "Oh, Lord, I'm so tired. I know you understand, so instead of driving all the way over to Radiant for service before I go open the store, I will take my Bible to the store and study Your Word all day, I promise." Well, I did take my Bible and I did study His Word all day, and it was about the second week of December that He revealed to me I was offering up excuses to Him and that skipping church service on Sunday was not going to be acceptable any longer! He also told me to *slow down, sit down, and shut up* for awhile. Well, you know what a person should do when He makes it that clear! So, it was *the* hardest day of my life, but I called the leader of the women's ministry and explained to her that I would not be able to continue to lead the Women's Bible Study after the first of the year because of my crazy schedule; and it was just too hard because we only have one vehicle and my husband has to work at the store all day during the week because I have a full-time job to deal with...It just got too hard for me to take him to work on Thursdays so I could have the truck to get to Bible study on Thursday nights...I would have to leave my house at 5:00 p.m. to get there by a little after 6:00 because of where I live and the traffic. It takes me thirty-five to forty minutes to get there with no traffic. I also knew I had to find a new church to attend on Sundays because I could never use the "poor me, I'm too tired" excuse again! My new church is only one mile from my house, so I went there for the first time that second Sunday in December. And I would not be telling the truth if I said I didn't have the spirit of comparison raging through my soul the first few weeks—OK, the first two months! It is an amazing house of God and so evident the entire property is [covered] and filled with the Holy Spirit...the pastor is awesome. But I missed *my* Radiant family so much, *my* Bible study class, *my* prayer team, *my* comfort zone.

Oh, God is so *good*! But I slowed down, I sat down, and I shut up—and I have been listening the last three months. My husband now works on Saturdays too so I can have one day off, we still only have one vehicle, we have met with an attorney to discuss bankruptcy, we are financially ruined, our marriage is strained, our dreams are shattered, our goals are so far out of sight we don't even really remember what they were, and each day seems to bring no relief to these issues...But this is where it gets so amazing. God is so faithful, and during the last three months of me slowing down, sitting down, and shutting up, He has held my hand tightly and drug me through a breakthrough! I now understand that meaning of "The truth will set

you free," and I now know that before it
sets you free it is going to hurt with a
pain that is unbearable and so deep that
it is the reason most good-hearted, well-
meaning Christians give up and ignore
the truth! I have learned that circumstances do not define who God is, and I
have learned what it truly means to walk
by faith and not by sight...I have learned
what it truly means to surrender.

Turns out the last five years that I
thought I was surrendered to Him I was
actually just using Him as my safety
net, or my trump card, if you will. I was
living like I could run off and do whatever I wanted to do or chase whatever I
wanted to chase because "I am a Christian and my heart is in the right place;
so if I get a wild hair to start a business,
I can do it and then ask Him to bless
it and He will." Oh, it sounds so funny
when I finally say it out loud like this.
I finally understand what it means to
give my life to Him and to die to myself
daily and take up my cross. I am *finally*
ready to live the life He has planned for

me instead of the one that I have been
desperately trying to create for myself!

My circumstances have not changed
in the last three months. Well, yes,
they have; they have gotten worse and
more serious, and I am standing at the
biggest crossroads I have ever faced
in my life. But for the very first time
I realize what real biblical joy means,
what being thankful in all circumstances means, that what He said
about, "We will have trouble in this
world"...wasn't kidding. And I realized
it's not about *me* and *my*.

We all have trouble and problems
and circumstances beyond our understanding or definition of *fair*. We all
carry a burden and a load of pain and
suffering every day. I'm not special,
I'm not different, but thank God I now
understand that I don't have to carry it
anymore and that He will bless my life
if I am seeking His blessings and not
mine! I was so busy trying to create
the perfect Christian life that poor God
didn't have a chance to interject or apply

His Word. I choked the Holy Spirit right out of my soul. God cannot move or work in someone's life when they are living like that. God works in and through the lives of His people that are completely surrendered to Him so that His power and His glory and His ways can be seen and understood. It's not my life, not my business, not my battle.

So, I'm stepping lightly and keeping my mouth shut and my ears open. I'm ready for His plan. I have no idea what is going to happen to my old plans but I don't care anymore. I know I have to wake up every day and do my best. I know I have to honor my contract and show up and open the doors, but I have no idea what His next move is going to be. It very well could be He allows us to file bankruptcy and start over with a clean slate, or it could be that He brings a miracle into our life to restore our finances and not have to go down that road. Or it could be neither, and He has something in store I can't even begin to dream up. But for the first time in my life, I'm totally relaxed and worry-free and excited to see what He is going to do—Him, not me.

Oh, thank you, Carolyn, for letting me pour this out to you. I could go on and on and on, because there are so many more layers and levels He has revealed, but I better get to work; and nobody likes getting novel e-mails. But speaking of books, where can I buy yours? I just cannot wait to get my hands on it.

Please tell me all about you and Bob and life and the book when you have time.

God bless you, my friend.

I love and miss you!

I had never received such an e-mail in all my life. Doesn't it blow your mind that it would come just as I was concluding this story?

I wanted to respond to my friend in such a way that would provide her encouragement, but I also wanted to give her hope that her newfound declarations would be taken seriously.

Golfers, at the end of each round, are responsible

for signing their own scorecards attesting to each score. Additionally, their playing partners hold them accountable, too, by signing their name to the card as well.

I was going to hold my friend accountable. Here is how I responded.

> Thank you so much for pouring out your thoughts. I am so very blessed to have a friend like you!
>
> Without realizing it, you have just confirmed the writings of my second book, *Eagle: Two Under Par and Soaring for God*. You are an amazing woman, and I will pray for your newfound freedom. This second book is about the people who are able to emulate Christ-like behavior. You may not understand much about golf, but being under par is a good thing. The emphasis of the book has to do with three key fundamentals in golf that we Christians need to hold on to.
>
> The keys are balance, keeping an eye on the ball, and aligning ourselves with the target, or in our case, with

Him. You have just managed to articulate all of those elements perfectly. God is so amazing that He would help you with this and that He would make you a part of this book. With your permission…I would like to reprint this e-mail as part of my concluding chapter in the book. What you have just written will be the most inspirational part of the entire book! You will have just helped hopefully thousands by what you have written.

Why had you been thinking about me, I wonder? Do you suppose God was nudging you to write and write the way you did so your story could be helpful to you, yes, but to others too?

I am overwhelmed in this moment dear friend…Wow. God is incredible!

I love you. Let me know what you are thinking.

Hang in there. I will pray. Thank you for being you!

All my love,
Carolyn

Here is her final response to me:

> I have goose bumps so big right now
> they are popping through my jeans!
> Carolyn, I'm just absolutely awestruck!
> First, because I am so proud and excited
> for you that you are writing your second
> book! Praise God...And second that
> He used me and my school of hard
> knocks degree to validate and confirm
> that *Eagle: Two Under Par and Soaring
> for God* is going to touch lives, change
> hearts, and light some fires for Christ!
>
> I am so incredibly honored and
> humbled that you would ask to use my
> writing...in your book. And this is also
> yet another confirmation and validation
> from Him, because to be honest with
> you, when I sat down to write to you I
> just said, "Come, Holy Spirit, come,"
> and I just let Him share my heart with
> you in His words, not mine. Whenever
> I do that I never go back and read the e-
> mail because I'm afraid I will be tempted
> to tweak it or add or subtract from it. I
> don't always ask the Holy Spirit to do

my e-mails for me (and hey, that could
be book three...because I should more
often!), but when I do, I trust Him.

One million thank yous!

I am so overwhelmed right now, too,
and just love, love, love how He works in
us and through us—when we get out of
the way!

My friend is an incredible eagle for Christ. She
totally gets it.

She is a natural encourager. Here she is in the
midst of personal chaos, and her first thought was
to ask about me, Bob, our health and happiness, and
how the first book may have impacted others. She
has learned what it means to have Him balancing
our lives and keeping Him in our focus despite our
personal tragedies.

To be sure, many of you are suffering greatly,
and I wonder if any one of us would have regarded
our circumstances as she did as "real biblical joy."
As an eagle, she is soaring for Him, as she realizes that it is He who provides her with flight!
She is responding with a commitment to fully
align herself in His direction. She has proclaimed
that she no longer cares for her "old plans." She is

"relaxed, worry-free, and excited to see what He is going to do."

Congratulations, my dear friend, for playing an under-par round for Christ! Thanks also to Nancy and Pastor Bill.

I shared with Bob God's incredible ending to this story. He said, "Why would you hear from her now? I wonder why she was thinking of you so much. You haven't heard from her in months. She had to go out of her way to contact you."

"I know," I said. "Isn't God amazing?"

"Yes, but what does she mean about being free in Him?" Bob asked. "I have heard pastor talk about that, but I just don't get it."

I didn't respond in the moment but later asked Bob to read this draft before sending it to Strang. I wrote the following, "Honey, if you didn't get God's message of freedom in *Mulligan* and if it hasn't been made apparent to you now with *Eagle*, well, you will just have to wait for the third book—*Ace: One in Golf and One with God*."

> "If you hold to my teaching, you are really my disciples. Then you will know the truth, and the truth will set you free."
> —John 8:31

ABOUT THE AUTHOR

AROLYN SNELLING AND her husband, Bob, live in Surprise, Arizona. She holds a bachelor's degree in human relations from the University of San Francisco and a master's of science degree in psychology. For seventeen years she worked in the secular world in both the human resources and public relations fields. For the last few years she has worked and volunteered in the Radiant Church ministry. Carolyn is the author of *Mulligan: A Second Chance at True Love and God's Grace.*

My beautiful family (from left to right): My hubby Bob, my grandson Cameron, my grandson Austin, my stepdaughter Teri, my granddaughter Stacy, and in back my son-in-law Terry!

TO CONTACT THE AUTHOR

www.heartofthecrossbooks.com

THE **G.O.L.F.**: **G**OD **O**UR **L**OVING **F**ATHER SERIES CONTINUES

Book 3: *Ace: One in Golf and One with God*—Coming in 2010

Book 4: *Fore: Four Spiritual Weapons for Christians*—Coming in 2011

First book in the G.O.L.F. Series

Mulligan:

A Second Chance at True Love and God's Grace

In golf, there's a term for a second chance— a mulligan—in which a golfer has the opportunity to retake an errant shot.

What do you wish you could do over?

After a failed first marriage, Carolyn Snelling knew that God had given her the best in the form of her second husband, Bob. In fact, he provided her with an example of Christ's unconditional love, which led her to a saving relationship with Jesus Christ. Through her new life in the Lord and her remarriage, Snelling has learned that the God she serves truly is a God of second chances.

ISBN-13: 978-1-59979-528-7